To

From

To Adam, with love   S.P.
To Mum, Dad and twin sister, Victoria   C.W.

Written and compiled by Sophie Piper
Illustrations copyright © 2009
Caroline Williams
This edition copyright © 2009
Lion Hudson

The right of Caroline Williams to be identified as the illustrator of this work has been asserted by her in accordance with the Copyright, Designs and Patents Act 1988.

All rights reserved. No part of this publication may be reproduced or transmitted in any form or by any means, electronic or mechanical, including photocopy, recording, or any information storage and retrieval system, without permission in writing from the publisher.

Published by Lion Children's Books
an imprint of
Lion Hudson plc
Wilkinson House, Jordan Hill Road,
Oxford OX2 8DR, England
www.lionhudson.com/lionchildrens
UK ISBN 978 0 7459 6184 2
US ISBN 978 0 8254 7914 4

First edition 2009

Acknowledgments
All unattributed prayers are by Sophie Piper, Lois Rock, Mary Joslin and Christina Goodings, copyright © Lion Hudson. Prayer by Victoria Tebbs is copyright © Lion Hudson.

A catalogue record for this book is available from the British Library

Printed and bound in China,
November 2013, LH17

Blessings for a

baby boy

•

Written and compiled by
Sophie Piper

Illustrated by
Caroline Williams

LION
CHILDREN'S

Welcome, baby

God bless you, darling baby boy,
whose life has just begun.
God keep you safe, so you may find
your own place in the sun.

Blessings for a baby boy

Little baby,
just awakened,
you are part of
God's creation.

Little baby,
oh, so small,
God is father
of us all.

Welcome, baby

Blessings for a baby boy

Welcome, baby

Bless my hair and bless my toes
Bless my ears and bless my nose
Bless my eyes and bless each hand
Bless the feet on which I stand
Bless my elbows, bless each knee:
God bless every part of me.

Blessings for a baby boy

Here are the tiny clothes,
Here are the toys.
Here is the baby
Who makes all the noise.

Hush! I am here with you,
Here I will stay
Watching you, loving you
Every day.

Welcome, baby

Blessings for a baby boy

How many days has my baby to play?
Saturday, Sunday, Monday,
Tuesday, Wednesday, Thursday, Friday,
Saturday, Sunday, Monday.

Traditional

Love

The sun may shine
The rain may fall
God will always
Love us all.

Victoria Tebbs

Little deeds of kindness,
Little words of love,
Help to make earth happy,
Like the heaven above.

Julia Carney (1823–1908)

Love

Love

God bless all those that I love;

God bless all those that love me;

God bless all those that love those that I love,

And all those that love those that love me.

From an old New England sampler

Blessings for a baby boy

Dear Father, hear and bless
Thy beasts and singing birds,
And guard with tenderness
Small things that have no words.

Traditional

Love

Blessings for a baby boy

Love

All things bright and beautiful,
All creatures great and small,
All things wise and wonderful,
The Lord God made them all.

Each little flower that opens,
Each little bird that sings,
He made their glowing colours,
He made their tiny wings.

Mrs Cecil Frances Alexander
(1818–95)

Moon and stars

Now the day is over,
Night is drawing nigh.
Shadows of the evening
Steal across the sky.

Now the darkness gathers,
Stars begin to peep,
Birds and beasts and flowers
Soon will be asleep.

Sabine Baring-Gould (1834–1924)

Blessings for a baby boy

I see the moon
And the moon sees me;
God bless the moon
And God bless me.

Traditional

Moon and stars

Moon and stars

Climb a silver ladder

To the moon above.

Pick a bowl of starlight

For the one you love.

Blessings for a baby boy

Little lambs, little lambs,
Where do you sleep?
'In the green meadow,
With Mother Sheep.'

Little birds, little birds,
Where do you rest?
'Close to our mother,
In a warm nest.'

Baby dear, baby dear,
Where do you lie?
'In my warm bed,
With Mother close by.'

Moon and stars

Blessings for a baby boy

Moon and stars

The moon shines bright,
The stars give light
Before the break of day;
God bless you all
Both great and small
And send a joyful day.

Traditional

God bless

Clouds in the sky above,
Waves on the sea,
Angels up in heaven
Watching over you and me.

Blessings for a baby boy

The little angels think it grand
To sit up through the night,
Watching you, dear baby boy,
Until the morning bright.

They make themselves all neat and clean
And feel so very proud
To bring their little teddies
And snuggle on a cloud.

They bring with them a box of dreams –
Good dreams of joy and love
That float like silver stardust
To earth from heaven above.

God bless

Blessings for a baby boy

God bless

Now I lay me down to sleep,
I pray thee, Lord, thy child to keep;
Thy love to guard me through the night
And wake me in the morning light.

Traditional

Blessings for a baby boy

Lord, keep us safe this night,
Secure from all our fears;
May angels guard us while we sleep,
Till morning light appears.

John Leland (1754–1841)

God bless

God bless

Lullaby and goodnight:
let the angels of light
spread their wings round your bed;
may they guard you from dread.
Slumber gently and deep
in the dreamland of sleep,
slumber gently and deep
in the dreamland of sleep.

Brahms lullaby

For a special photo